About this book

Everyone knows the legends of Ancient Greece. Hercules and his tasks, the wooden horse of Troy and the travels of Odysseus are still popular and exciting stories. But what was real life like? If you had been a Greek boy or girl over two thousand years ago, would you have gone to school? What would you have eaten for dinner? Were there toys and games for playtime? What clothes would you have worn?

Amanda Purves takes us back to those far-off days and describes life at home, at school, at work and at play. Pictures of beautiful buildings, vases and jewels – as well as everyday objects – help us to understand why this ancient civilization was so great. The Greeks were good thinkers, writers and politicians, too. You may be surprised at how modern their life was, long before the birth of Christ!

Some of the words printed in *italics* may be new to you. You can look them up in the word list on page 92.

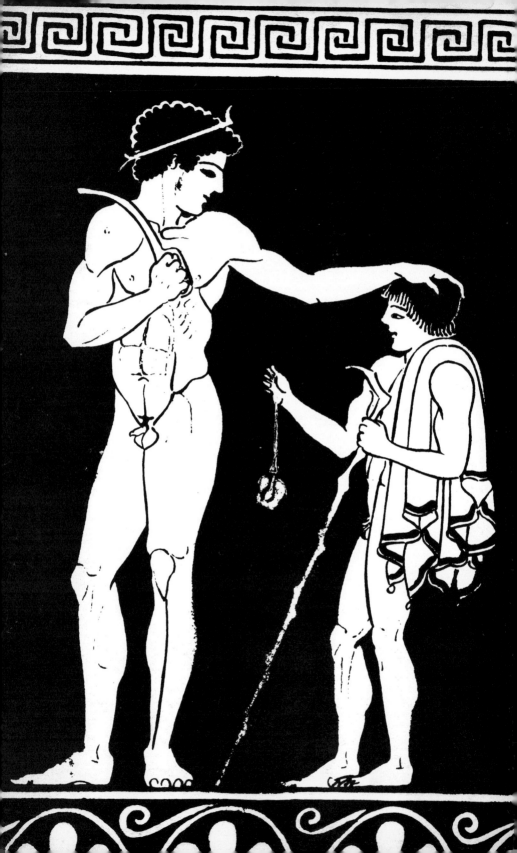

Growing up in Ancient Greece

AMANDA PURVES

EASTERN SHORE PUBLIC LIBRARY
ACCOMAC, VIRGINIA 23301

Wayland

Growing up in Other Times

Frontispiece:
A young boy helping an athlete
to prepare for the Olympic Games.

ISBN 0 85340 541 7
Copyright © 1978 by Wayland (Publishers) Ltd
First published in 1978 by Wayland (Publishers) Ltd,
49 Lansdowne Place, Hove, East Sussex, BN13 1HF, England
Text set in 12 pt. VIP Univers by Trident Graphics, Reigate
Printed in Great Britain by Gale and Polden Ltd, Aldershot, and bound by
The Pitman Press Ltd, Bath

Contents

1. Family Life

From carvings that we can still see today, it seems that the Ancient Greeks were kind parents. We do not know very much about the early life of children except that their parents and nurses spent a lot of time preparing them for growing up. Girls and their mothers led very restricted lives by today's standards. They were expected only to be good daughters and wives and to look after their menfolk. A few women worked outside the home as priestesses or temple dancers. Women could not vote or take part in public life at all.

Of course boys had a much better time. They were encouraged to be brave and independent. Boys who grew up in Athens had to learn a trade when they were fifteen. They also had to serve in the army or navy for at least two years when they were eighteen.

Life was very comfortable for the Ancient Greeks. Almost every family had slaves. The number varied according to how well off the family was. Even children had their own slaves. But in poor families, especially those farming in the countryside, everyone had to work hard as soon as they were old enough.

Childbirth

To us, these ways of helping a woman having a baby seem cruel. The Greeks thought that if a pregnant woman was lifted up and down the baby would come more quickly. When a boy was born, an olive wreath was hung on the door to show it was good news. Girls weren't so welcome. If a baby was unwanted, it was left outside and anyone who found it could keep it. Many babies and young children died because the doctors didn't know how to cure their illnesses. The picture of children playing comes from a baby's tomb.

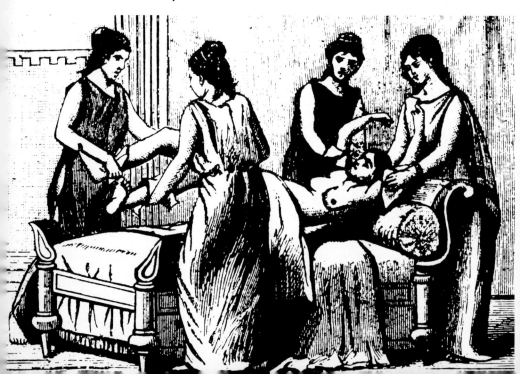

Clothes Some children, like this little boy taking a thorn out of his foot, didn't wear anything! Most children wore simple, cool tunics made out of a big sheet. Boys usually wore a knee-length

white *chiton,* but girls' tunics were long and bright. Workmen had brown ones that didn't show the dirt. In winter, Greeks wore cloaks and sandals or backless shoes. But not underwear!

Cleanliness The Ancient Greeks were very clean people. Here you can see women washing at an enormous basin and taking showers. At the public baths there were separate rooms for boys and girls. As there was no soap, they rubbed olive oil into their skins and then scraped it off (and the dirt) with special sticks.

Beauty You can see the different hair styles Greek women liked. Some of them are so complicated that they must have taken ages to do every morning. Banded headdresses were popular as well. Both men and women perfumed their hair. Some Greek women wore make-up. Ischomachus tells how his wife once put chalk on her face to make it whiter and berry juice on her lips. He didn't like the result very much! Men were vain, too, and took great care over their appearance. Even children were expected to look beautiful.

Slaves Household slaves were kindly treated by the Greeks. They were always foreigners and often prisoners of war. The Greeks bought new ones in the market. This slave is tying on his mistress's sandal. There were slaves to do everything. Because slaves did all the work, the Ancient Greeks could spend a lot of time having fun.

14

Weddings   Marriages were arranged by parents. Girls married at about fifteen years old but boys often waited until they were thirty. Before her wedding, a Greek girl gave her toys to the temple, to show that her childhood had ended. She also had a bath to wash off her old life. Her father gave a party and then the bride was led, wearing a veil, to her new home by a procession of friends. They showered her and her bridegroom with fruit and grain for luck.

Funerals The Greeks thought the dead went to Hades "where dwell the phantoms of men outworn". The dead person had a coin placed under his or her tongue, to pay the fare for the journey to Hades. Flasks of wine and honey cakes were placed with the body to make sure it was not hungry. Then it was carried on a bier, accompanied by hired mourners and flute players, and cremated. The ashes were buried in an urn, with some of the dead person's possessions. Some families had splendid tombs like this one.

2. The Greek Home

The Greek children did not spend much time in their houses because it was too hot for most of the year. They used them mainly for eating and sleeping in. The rooms were airy and cool, with very little furniture.

Farmers in the country lived in simple huts, made from sun-baked mud, with thatched roofs. Town houses were usually built on wooden frames, filled in with mud, and had tiled roofs. They were often two storeys high, with shutters to keep out the sun but no glass in the windows. The house in the picture belonged to quite a wealthy family. There is a long, columned front to give shade. Inside there were separate rooms for living and sleeping.

Although the Greeks were not very interested in their houses, they took great care over their pottery. Ancient Greek pottery is famous for its beauty. It was used for everything from jars for storing olives to delicate perfume bottles. Many of the vases are decorated with stories of heroes and gods, or scenes from everyday life. Fortunately, they made so many that lots of Greek vases are on display in museums all over the world today.

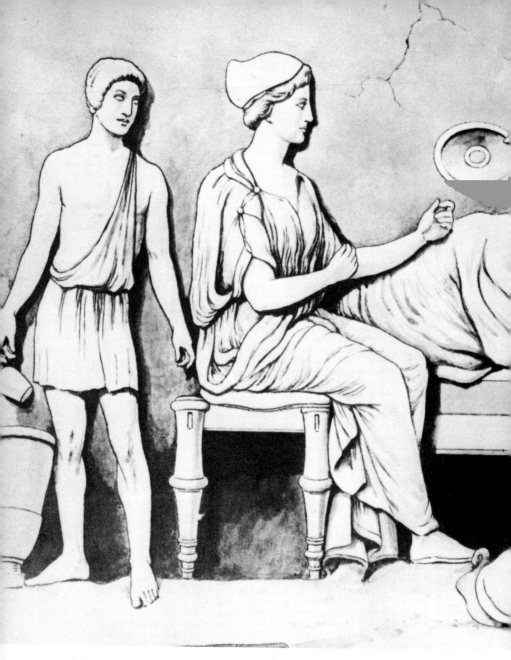

Meals Greek meals were very lazy affairs. You can see that the father is reclining while he eats. His wife has a stool but the children often had to stand, or to sit on the floor. Greeks didn't eat much meat unless they had sacrificed an animal to

20

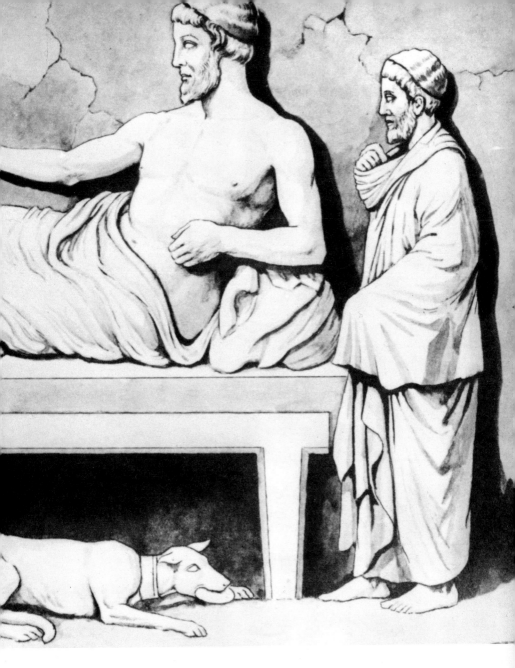

their gods. They liked fish and black pudding, but more often they ate peas, porridge, bread and delicious crumbly goats' cheese. There was lots of fresh fruit, such as grapes and figs. For a treat, they had honey cakes.

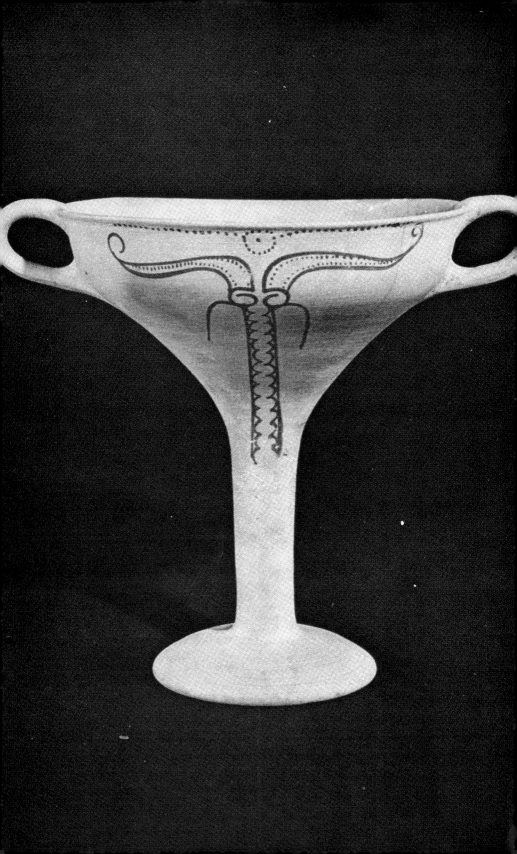

Wine Everyone, including children, drank lots of wine. It was always mixed with plenty of water. Only foreigners drank it neat. Women did most of the work in the vineyards — hoeing, pruning and harvesting the grapes. When the wine was made by treading the juice out of the grapes, it was stored in two-handled *amphoras* like this. The Greeks drank out of pottery cups. This bull cup has no stem and can't stand up. The drinker had to finish his wine in one gulp! The other cup was made over three thousand years ago.

Furniture The most useful pieces of furniture in a Greek house were couches for eating and for sleeping. You can see some other furniture in the pictures in this chapter — a stool, a chair and a table. Food was usually eaten from three-legged tables. Babies had high-chairs made out of clay. The Greeks stored their clothes in chests or cupboards but everything else was hung on hooks on the walls. Wealthy families decorated their houses with tapestries, vases on stands and statues of members of the family.

Pottery We have already seen some uses for pottery. The Greeks also cooked in it, stored oil in it, ate from it, and cooled and heated water in it. You can tell Greek pottery by the black or red paintings which dance around the sides. The picture of a girl being pushed on a swing by a *satyr* (woodland god) comes from a vase. You will see lots more vase paintings in this book. See if you can recognize them. The little pottery perfume bottles with sprinkler tops were made on the island of Rhodes about 600 BC.

Spinning It was the job of the women and girls to make the family's clothes. They must have spent long hours spinning and weaving to make the fine wool cloth. This lady is winding wool around her leg before beginning to spin. After spinning the wool, she would weave it on an upright loom.

Toys Greek children had plenty to keep them occupied at home. Country children often had pets, such as dogs, geese and pigs. Remember the dog under the couch in the family meal picture? They had plenty of toys to choose from. The doll looks rather like our puppets. Sadly, the chariot overleaf was found in a child's tomb. Its owner can't have had much time to play with it.

3. Schools and Scrolls

Greeks thought that every boy should go to school and be educated. Boys started going to school when they were seven years old, if they came from wealthy families. Poor boys couldn't go to school at all because parents had to pay fees to the teacher. A slave took children to school and stayed with them all day, just to make sure that they behaved. But a girl's place was definitely in the home. She learned her skills from her mother.

The Ancient Greeks thought that they were very well-educated. They laughed at foreigners for the way they spoke. It all sounded like "bar-bar" to the Greeks, so they called foreigners *barbarians.* But Greeks really were very advanced thinkers. Greek philosophers were famous for their ideas about unanswerable questions. "What is the point of life?" and "How did the world get here?" were the sort of problems they thought about in the fourth and fifth centuries before Christ.

Today we still study Greek philosophers. Some of our buildings copy the beautiful columns of Ancient Greek architecture. We watch Greek plays in our theatres. At school we learn Greek mathematics. And we have taken our ideas of government from the Ancient Greeks, too.

Writing Schoolchildren wrote on wax-coated tablets made out of wood. This teacher is scratching words on to a tablet with a stylus. One end of the stylus is pointed for writing with. The other end is blunt for rubbing out mistakes. The man with the beard and the long stick is the boy's slave. He's keeping a firm eye on the boy!

Scrolls and Letters This teacher is holding a scroll for his pupil to read. Scrolls were books. They were made up of lots of pages joined together and then rolled up. You can see that some of the letters of the Greek alphabet are the same as ours, and some are different. Greeks still use this alphabet today but they no longer write from right to left. The Romans copied many of their letters from the Greeks, and we copied them from the Romans.

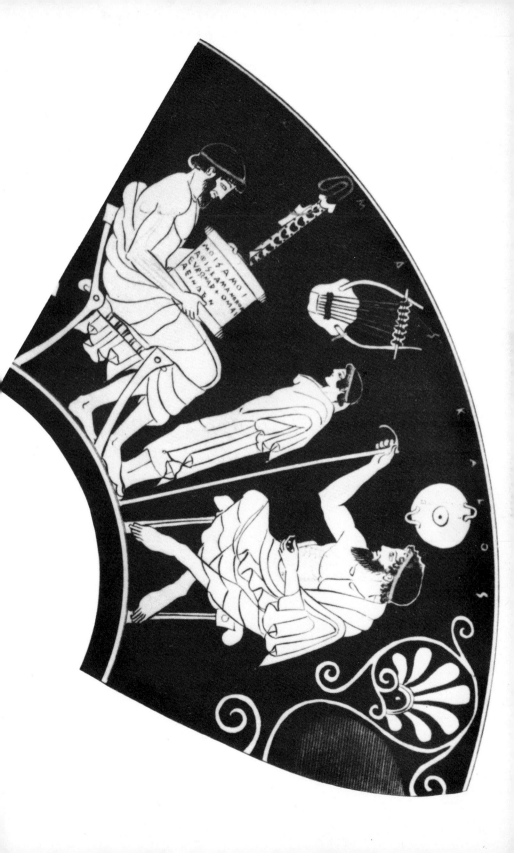

Maths Greeks learned to count on an *abacus.*
This is a wooden frame with rows of beads on it.
The Greeks used the letters of the alphabet for
writing numbers, too. They thought that numbers
were very important and even magical. They
measured and counted when building, and liked
everything to be a regular shape. Here is a sundial
made by a mathematician called Phaedrus and a
pair of bronze compasses.

41

Philosophers The most famous Greek thinkers were Socrates, Plato and Aristotle. They lived in Athens about four hundred years before Christ. These pictures show you philosophers teaching in Athens. The garden where they are instructing their pupils is called the academic grove. The building is the academy, which is the college or university.

Music You will see lots of pictures of people playing musical instruments in this book. Greeks listened to music at feasts, danced to it and also recited poetry to it. Here you can see a boy learning to play the lyre, a stringed instrument that was plucked, rather like a small harp. Flutes and pipes were also popular. Perhaps the boy in the other picture is reciting the poetry he has learned as his teacher plays his double pipe.

Sport Greeks thought sport was just as important as learning to read and write. Boys didn't learn to play cricket or football but they knew other ball games. They learned to wrestle and to use weapons, too. The greatest honour for a boy who liked sport was to be chosen to take part in the Olympic Games. Here a boy is watching his teacher demonstrating the way to long-jump. Athletes oiled their bodies and scraped their skin afterwards. You can see the oil-holder on the wall and the scrapers in the boy's hands.

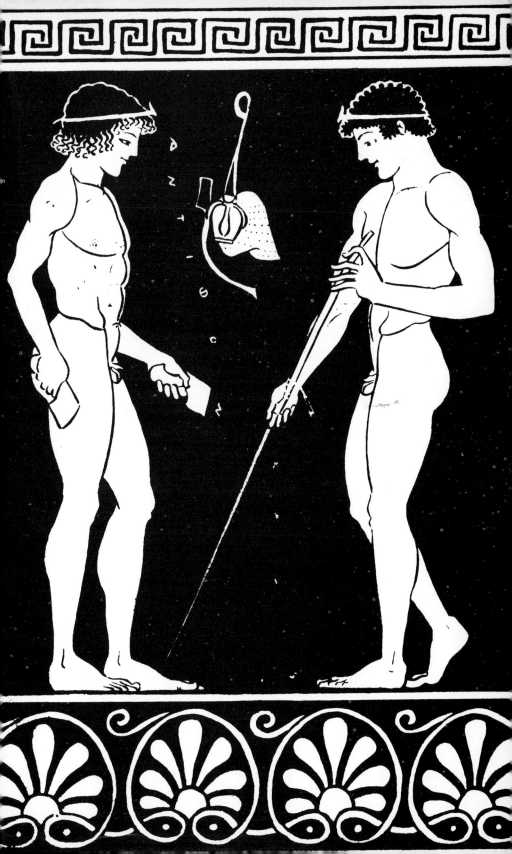

Spartan Schools Sparta was a part of Greece where parents made sure their children were really fit. Boys were examined every ten days to check that they hadn't put on any weight! They went to boarding schools, where they

learned only physical education. This meant not
only wrestling, but also knowing how to bear cold,
hunger and pain. Spartan boys were disciplined
and obedient. They made very good soldiers. Boys
could join the army when they were seven years old.

Girls Greek girls were left at home. They learned from their mothers how to be good wives. A girl had to spend her childhood "under the strictest restraint, in order that she may see as little, hear as little and ask as few questions as possible". It doesn't sound much fun. But Spartan girls had to be fit. This one is having a good sprint!

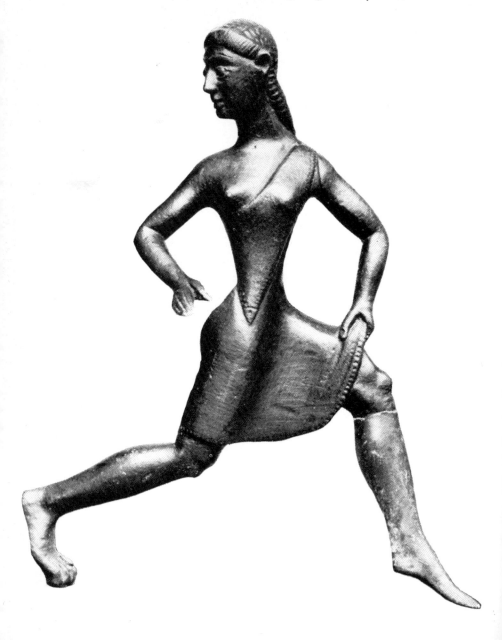

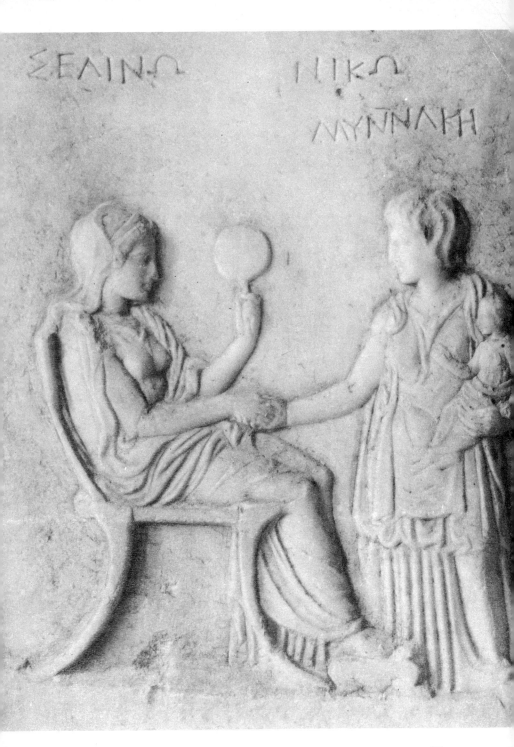

4. Gods and Goddesses

The Ancient Greeks' religion may seem strange — they did not believe in only one god but worshipped many. They thought their gods lived on Mount Olympus and looked down on them to make sure that they behaved. To keep the gods in a good mood, the Greeks built beautiful temples for them and made sacrifices to them. Before meals, mothers sacrificed wine or cakes to the family god. At dinner parties, wine was often spilled onto the floor as a sacrifice. The Athenians worshipped Athene, the goddess of wisdom. But other parts of Greece had their own favourite gods and goddesses.

Many legends sprang up about the gods and heroes of Ancient Greece. You probably know some of them. Have you heard the story of Jason and the Argonauts, or Perseus and the Gorgon? Or the tales about Odysseus, composed by the poet Homer around 800 BC? Ancient Greek children listened to their parents or friends telling these tales. Not everyone believed them. But they did believe in their gods, and people who were disrespectful to them were punished.

In this picture, you can see the gods Zeus and Apollo at the top. The man being crowned at the bottom is the poet Homer.

The Gods The Greeks had gods and goddesses for everything, from corn to blacksmiths. Zeus was the father of the gods. This marble carving shows the wedding of Zeus and Hera. Zeus's two brothers were important gods, too. Hades was the god of the underworld, where the dead souls went. And Poseidon was the god of the sea. You may also have heard of Apollo, the god of light; Hermes, the messenger of the gods; and Aphrodite, the goddess of love.

Acropolis and Parthenon

The word *acropolis* means fortress or high city. The most famous is this one, built in Athens. Most of the buildings are in ruins, but it is still a very impressive sight. The best-known building on the Acropolis is the Parthenon. It took ten years to build this temple. It's dedicated to Athene, of course. There used to be a huge statue of her inside the temple, watching over the city.

Oracles Hundreds of Greek families flocked to Delphi each year to visit the most famous of the country's 250 *oracles*. These were places where you could ask the gods for advice. Delphi was dedicated to Apollo, god of prophecy and light. The temple is now in ruins, but you can see its remains. A priest led a goat to the temple and sprinkled it with water. If the goat didn't move, it meant that Apollo didn't want to speak. But if the goat did move, Apollo would answer questions. A priestess did the talking! This father with his two sons is asking Apollo's advice.

Temples The Greeks built temples as homes for the gods. All the temples were very beautiful, with columns and carvings. But not many were as big as the Parthenon or as often visited as the Temple of Apollo at Delphi. Most were small and simple, like this one. It is called the Temple of Victory and it can still be seen in Athens.

Sacrifices The Greeks didn't have services in their temples. They gave their gods presents to keep them happy. Sometimes they killed animals and gave parts to the gods, eating the rest themselves. Mothers would give wine and cakes to the gods before family meals, rather like saying grace. This potter is offering his first pieces of work – the two bowls in his hand – to his goddess.

Dionysus The festival of Dionysus, god of wine and revelry, was held in August to give thanks for the grape harvest. His followers often dressed up as satyrs. They are the people with tails in these pictures. Sometimes they became so excited that they did crazy dances and even attacked and ate wild animals and children. Dionysus also gave comfort to suffering people and assured them that there was life after death.

5. Fun and Games

The Ancient Greeks liked having fun. Children played many of the games that we enjoy, such as blind man's buff, skittles and marbles. Their parents enjoyed having dinner parties and listening to poetry and music.

Of course there were no cinemas to visit or televisions to watch. But there were plenty of other things to go and see. The theatre was fun, though very different from ours. Sporting events were popular, too. Most famous of all were the Olympic Games.

The first known Olympic Games took place in 776 BC. After that, they were held every four years, always at the foot of Mount Olympus as part of a festival for Zeus. The Games lasted for five days but for a whole month war was forbidden so that even enemies could take part. Men flocked from every corner of Greece, either to take part or to watch. Women had their separate games. There was lots to keep everyone amused, and hundreds of stalls provided food, drink and souvenirs.

Many of the events in today's Olympic Games are the same as three thousand years ago. But of course they are held in different parts of the world and athletes from many nations take part.

Children's Games These girls are playing knucklebones, a very popular children's game in Ancient Greece. It was played with the shin bones of sheep. The five knucklebones were thrown into the air and caught on the back of the hand. We play variations of this game today called fives or jacks. Greek children also liked playing with balls and hoops.

66

Theatres All the family enjoyed going to the theatre to see tragedies by Euripedes and Sophocles, or comedies by Aristophanes. These playwrights lived nearly five hundred years before Christ but their plays are still performed today. Our theatres are more comfortable, though! Ancient Greek theatres were open-air. The wooden seats went up in semi-circular rows so that everyone had a good view of the stage. The audience brought their own cushions to sit on. This Ancient Greek theatre in Athens is still in use.

Cockfighting We think cock-fighting is very cruel and it is illegal in many countries. But it was a popular sport in Ancient Greece. As you can see from the picture, two cocks were made to fight each other until one was killed. The Greeks put bets on the one they thought would win.

Boxers and Wrestlers Greek boxing gloves were very different from Muhammad Ali's. Can you see the special straps the boxer is wearing to strengthen his arms and make his punches more painful? Wrestling was popular with the crowd. Everyone yelled out advice. Two other people are pushing and prodding these wrestlers to make sure they keep fighting.

The Olympic Games

The most exciting entertainments of all were the Olympic Games. It was the dream of every athlete to take part. The vase picture above shows you an athlete getting ready to compete. One is putting oil on his hands to make them supple. Another is having his feet inspected. The statue of the discus thrower shows that it isn't as simple as spinning a frisbee. The discus could weigh as much as 4 kg (9 lbs). An athlete who won an event was awarded a crown of laurels as his prize. Sometimes the crown was gilded to make it last longer.

DISCOBOLO
DI MIR

Dinner Parties Greeks were very fond of wine
and good food. At their dinner parties they ate
shrimp, octopus, thrushes in honey and roast
duck, with hunks of bread to mop up the juices,
followed by cheese, fruit and honeycombs. Lyre
players and acrobats entertained the guests bet-
ween courses. After dinner they played games or
told riddles. Those who couldn't solve the riddles
had to drink wine mixed with salt. This is not the
sort of party which children would have been
invited to!

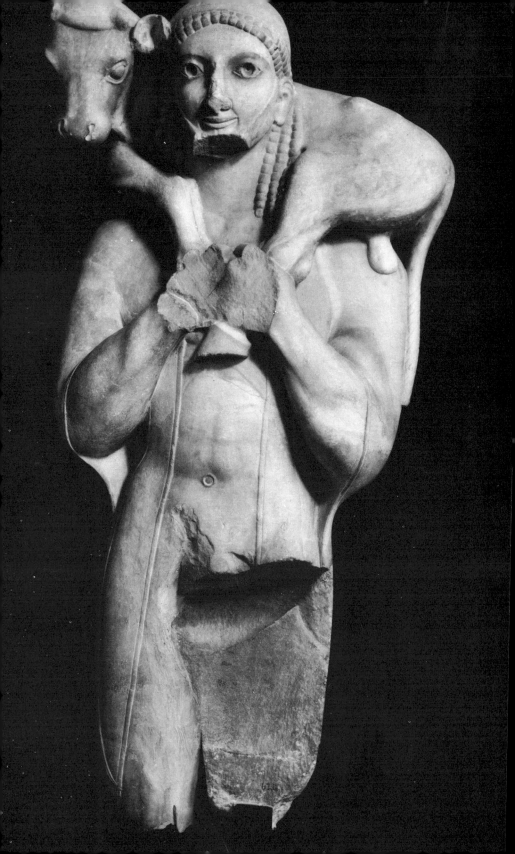

6. Town and Country

Greece was made up of several city-states. Each one had its own capital, army and coins. They often fought each other. Athens was the largest.

Any citizen could make a speech at the weekly meeting about how the city should be run. Everyone had the vote – except women, foreigners and slaves. They called this democracy. It means government by the people, or by politicians chosen by the people. In time of war, every adult man had to fight for his city-state. They had to pay for their own armour and food, so poor people were not too keen on war.

Life in the towns was busy and exciting. Smiths, carpenters and potters made and sold their wares. In Athens, boys became apprentices at the age of fifteen and learned a trade. But in the country most people were farmers. Their year started with pruning the vines and weeding. In April and May the wheat was ready for harvesting. Then in August or September the grapes ripened, followed by the olives. Wheat and barley were sown in autumn. When there was time, the women spun wool and the families made oil, wine and cheese.

The Agora An Ancient Greek town square was called an *agora.* This is what the agora in Athens may have looked like. You can see stalls selling all kinds of goods. Flower sellers displayed poppies, irises and garlands. Fruit sellers sold figs, grapes and peaches. Here slaves were for sale, too. Adults went to the agora for haircuts, to read the government notices and to attend town meetings. Sometimes they went just for a gossip. Children enjoyed the performing conjurors and magicians.

Smiths Greek artists and craftsmen were very important. The men in this picture are bronze-smelters. The furnace is on the left. On the right, a craftsman is putting the finishing touches to a bronze statue. The Greeks used bronze a lot. Some examples of bronze-smelters' work, and their tools, are in this painting, too. The drawing shows a potter at work.

Doctors The Greeks often consulted the oracles about their health. Some oracles had hospitals attached and became health resorts, with mineral water cures. But city doctors, like this one examining a little boy, had clinics where they set bones and gave herbal medicines. The drawing shows Hippocrates, the most famous Greek doctor. He lived about 400 BC. You may have heard of the Hippocratic oath, which doctors still take today. Part of it is: "I will prescribe treatment to the best of my ability and judgement for the good of the sick."

Coins Every city-state had its own silver coins. Athens' emblem was an owl. The other coins have heads of Greek heroes. Which one do you think is Alexander the Great? Merchants often brought back coins from other city-states. They could change them for their own currency at a stall in the agora.

Soldiers Rich men who joined the army were called *hoplites.* They could afford to buy helmets, breast-plates, shields, spears and swords. Greeks were good soldiers. Boys in the city-state of Sparta could join the army at seven years old. On the next four pages you will see more pictures of soldiers, and a man helping his son put on his armour.

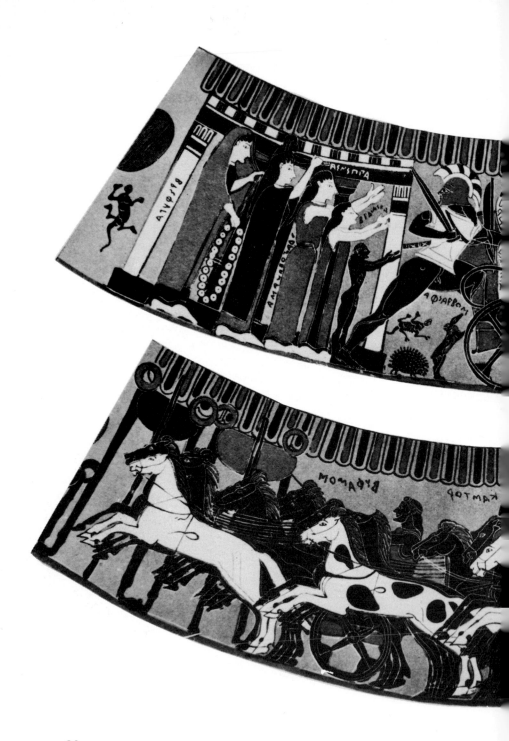

Sailors Ships were needed for war and for trading with other countries. This Athenian galley has a big sail but it still needed forty or fifty men to row it. Rowers were either poor men who could not afford to join the army, or slaves. Notice the stripes across the sail. They are made from bands of leather to make it stronger.

Farmers Everyone worked hard on a farm, even if there were slaves. Farmers' children were expected to help. They would look after the flocks, pick and tread grapes and join in harvesting. One of the most tiring jobs on the farm was grinding

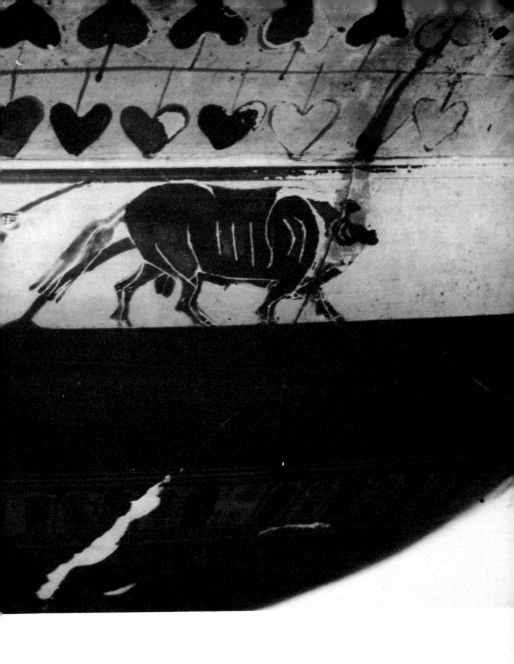

the grain into flour by hand. Children often worked as hard as the slaves. If you were growing up in Ancient Greece, you would probably choose to be a potter, an Olympic athlete or a soldier rather than a farmer!

New Words

Abacus	A wooden counting frame with rows of beads
Acropolis	The Greek word for "high city" or "fortress". "The Acropolis" usually means the hilltop buildings in Athens
Agora	A market square
Amphora	A jar with two handles, used for storing liquids
Barbarian	The Greek word for foreigners. We now use it for uncivilized people
Chiton	A garment made out of a single piece of cloth
Hoplite	A rich soldier who fought on foot
Lyre	A stringed instrument, plucked like a harp
Oracle	A place for consulting the gods. The most famous was at Delphi
Philosopher	Someone who seeks wisdom, a thinker
Satyr	A woodland god with a man's body, pointed ears and a tail

Ancient Greece (Macdonald Educational, 1957). An excellent book, very clearly presented and good for all ages.

Everyday Things in Ancient Greece by M & C H B Quennell (Batsford, 1954). A very detailed account of everything Greek. Most suitable for the older reader interested in archaeology.

The Greek People by E K Milliken (Harrap, 1952). Everything you need to know about Ancient Greece. A very detailed book, for older readers.

The Greeks by M Grant and D Pottinger (Nelson, 1968). A step-by-step Greek history, well set-out and full of information.

The Greeks (Macdonald Educational, 1957). Packed with detail and lots of colourful and lively pictures. Good for all ages.

They Lived Like This in Ancient Greece by M Neurath and J Ellis (Parrish, 1968). A very good starting book, full of good drawings and easy to read.

(Some of these books may be out of print and obtainable only from libraries.)

Index

Picture Credits

The author and publishers wish to thank all those who have given permission for copyright pictures to be reproduced on the following pages: The Mansell Collection, *frontispiece*, 6, 8 *top*, 12, 13, 15, 16, 17, 26–27, 28–29, 31, 32–33, 34, 36–37, 38, 39, 40, 41, 44, 45, 46, 47, 51, 54, 61, 63, 64 *top and bottom*, 68–69, 70, 71, 72, 73, 75, 76, 79 *top*, 81, 83, 84, 85, 86–87, 90–91, 93; Mary Evans Picture Library 14, 18, 24, 25, 42, 43, 48–49, 78; The Trustees of the British Museum, 22, 23 *right*, 27 *bottom*, 50, 52, 62, 66, 82 *top*; Radio Times Hulton Picture Library, 8 *bottom*, 9, 20–21, 59 *top*; Fotomas Index, 10, 23 *left*; Peter Clayton, 82 *bottom*; National Tourist Office of Greece, 55, 56–57, 58, 59 *bottom*, 60, 67. The remaining pictures are the property of the Wayland Picture Library.